Recovering from

My Addiction

Of

Nicotine

Can I quit Smoking?

By

Bruce D. Smith

My

Own

Personal Story

January 30, 2004

Revised May 2013

Hello, my name is Bruce D. Smith

Let me start by saying if you don't smoke now listen to what I have to say in here. Don't pick up that first cigarette!! Danger! Danger! Danger!

I had to put that in here because I had only wish I knew how bad smoking is to the health of everyone, even to those who do not even smoke. Yes you may ask how that can be. Well have you ever hear of second hand smoke? That is where you are smoking and the person next to you is breathing in the smoke from you.

As for my story it starts with my mother and father. They both smoked for years; however my mother quit when I was about 15 years old. She caught a very bad cold one winter she couldn't even breathe not less smoke. My father that was another case. Let's say he smoked all the way on to the day he died. Yes he paid for it. He died suddenly at the age of 61. He lay down to take a nap and just never woke up. According to the doctor he had a massive heart attack.

I was young when I had my first cigarette. I remember my friend and I would get a pack of cigarettes, go behind our old school then smoke the whole pack before we left. I was only twelve years old at the time. I didn't do this often; but for my friend this was when he was to become a smoker.

Well I turned that magic age of eighteen. At the time it was suppose to be the time of being legal of doing the things which you couldn't being underage. Just two examples was smoking and drinking. My friend was legal age also. This meant time to hit the bars. Well that was another mistake of mine I had made. That was when I started to smoke. My friend would ask me from time to time if I wanted a cigarette and I would take one off him. Boy would I get a buzz off my first one. As a matter of fact this is what entice me to start it not the addiction of that nasty habit. Boy did my life take a turn to the worse when that so called magic age came. I started to buy my own packs of smokes. I would leave my house thirty minutes early for work so I could get in two or three cigarettes in. I use to like this because I would get that buzz and when I lost it I would want it all over again. Sadly to say this was short lived. Within a week that buzz Ii would get from having that first cigarette was no longer, it was gone. By now I was addicted to them. They had the power over me. After a while I didn't care about anything but my cigarettes or alcohol. I knew my health was deterating as time went by. I was gaining weight very gact, getting sick with bronchitis a lot. I would get light headed a lot and felt dizzy from time to time especially when I would come down with bronchitis. I got laid off from my job in 1983 for about six months. You would think because of money I would cut back on things but I didn't, it just got worse. I did collect unemployment; however I didn't care. I still went out and drank and smoked. I would try to quit many times and many different ways. I remember two different ways. The first was hypnosis. I paid a psychologist $125.00 for half hour each session. This was back in the 80's mind you. I did even fall under. You must be wondering did it work. For me it did not work. I cannot say if this will be the same for someone else, each person is different. It may help someone. Then there was a staple in the ear. Again this cost me the same, $125.00. There was a medical doctor and he would put a staple in the ear using what else but a staple. The thing I would have to do was whenever I had an urge for a smoke I just pulled on my ear lobe and it was suppose to release some type of chemical from the body going to my brain. This would ease the urge to smoke. If it was out there I tried it. The one think I tried was the NIcDerm CQ patch. This was the best thing that helped me. I would go without a cigarette for weeks but then I would fall back into that nasty habit.

It was in the early 90's and I found a counselor who helped out nicotine addicts. He had some type of program to help. I was terribly sick and didn't know what was wrong with me. He felt it was due to my smoking. My mother didn't feel too good about him so I didn't continue with him. I wish I did though later in years.

I was smoking anywhere from two to three packs of cigarettes a day. I was a chain smoker, one after the other. I think it was finally catching up to my body, it was September 24, 1990, I felt as though I had no oxygen. I went home from work when I first went in. The closer I got home the worse if felt. Finally I just couldn't do it anymore. I pulled over into a gas station and ask them to call for an ambulance. I was taken in and checked out. They could not find anything wrong with me. I got off the emergency room bed and my legs felt like rubber. It felt like I was going to calasp on the spot. The was to be the beginning of a long, long illness.

I went to doctors for three years and went through many different tests. I finally went to a neurogist and one of his post diagnoses was post esphilaitis. He had me admitted to the hospital one time and found arsenic in my system. When he told me this I really started to wonder if my mother and sister were trying to kill me. Needless to say that was not the case. Back in the 90's doctors didn't know that was just one of the poisons found in smoking. He also diagnosed me with Chronic Fatigue Syndrome. This was so sever I ended up having to go on permanent disability.

Well time goes by and I was still getting spells. I kept running back and forth to the emergency room. I either drove myself or go by ambulance pending on how bad it was. It felt like sometimes I was going to pass out, sweats, rapid heart beats, chest pains and more. All I would hear from the doctors, "You need to quit smoking."

I was being treated by a pschycirists after I was admitted to the hospital. Then a friend of ours worked for a woman who works with people with Chronic Fatigue Syndrome. So I started to see her. I wasn't getting anywhere with the pscyhisst but just hiding my symptoms. My counselor knew of a doctor who also worked with people especially with CFS. He was about 1 ½ hours away from me but I thought it would be worth it. He was a very good doctor. Once again I had to have a lot of test done. One thing he found in my blood was called polyslysemia. This I where there are too many red blood cells and not enough white blood cells. The white bloods cells are the ones that carry oxygen through our system. The doctor told me this was due to smoking. I would have to go ever two weeks and have blood taken out of me. I would have to go back for blood test every two weeks so see how my blood levels were. Well they were always high. So what did this mean, yes I would have to go back and get more blood taken out. You know back then with all the things the doctors did find I wasn't convinced enough that it was due to my smoking. I was smoking from two to three packs a day sometimes even more. It would depend on how long I was awake. I think I was keeping the cigarette companies in business. I stayed with this doctor for about a year or so. I had to stop seeing him because of insurance. I could not afford the co-pay any longer. When I quit my job I was given insurance for a certain amount of time.

My illness got worse. It would get to the point whre I couldn't even sit or stand. It felt like I was getting electric shocks in my system. I think my nervous system was being overloaded I would say. Whenever I would lie down then I felt better. I would eat lunch standing up, not sitting in the chair. This truly was a living night mare. I never thought I would get better. It seems like after a few weeks being in the hospital I would start to feel better. Then I would be released. I would go into a partial day program where I would attend Monday thru Friday from 9am to 3pm. This would run just for six weeks then at the end of the six weeks I would be sent over to their outpatient department. Well I would be out of the hospital for about three maybe four months then next thing you know it and I was having the same type of spells. I would have to go thru it all over again. Doctors didn't realize how serious of a problem I had with the smoking. Yea sure they told me I should quit smoking however they never said this case. Actually I myself don't think back then they knew that smoking did all of this stuff which we know of today. See today looking back at my habit and my hospitalizations I would be home and smoking my usual two to three packs every day. Then after three maybe four months this would poison my system that I couldn't take it any longer. I would get so depressed, at times suicidal because not knowing what was wrong with me. The worst thing that bothered me each time my illness flared up was realizing that I am not over my illness. The question was, "would I ever be well?' My answer to me was, "no." I felt as though my life was coming to an end, never going to get better or over this horrible illness.

One thing I did not give up on and that I was trying to quit. I liked the patch system. I would wear it and use it for a while then one slip, back to the habit I fell. The key thing though no matter how many times I tried to stop, I never stop trying to quit.

Now July of 1999 came and my mother passed away just like my father, suddenly. I took her to have a cat scan one day and while having the test she slipped into a coma. Within two hours she died and I was at her side.

So these prompt my sister and me to move back to New Jersey. This was a blessing in dicised. I was set up with a new pscyrits and counselor. When I met the counselor he recommended me to attend their partial day center. I would go from Monday thru Friday, 9am to 3pm. Basically there would be different types of groups such as depression, anger, loss and so on. So now was my time to work on my illness, to combat it firsthand. One day when I was over there I found this brochure about nicotine addictions. Of course that grabbed my attention right away. I read it and it was about a counselor whom helps those with addictions. One of his specialties was nicotine addictions. I read more about it then I thought to myself I could never afford this. Then to my amazing eyes I saw, "we take people on a sliding scale." This was the opening to me. I called them to see if I qualified for their program and I did. This was the beginning of what I didn't know would be a new life of freedom.

I started my first day of counseling and we just didn't talk about my smoking but everything.

I tried my own business selling costume jewelry at our local flea market. I would make the gold plated chains for the people pending on the size they would want. This was not an easy task. I needed to have a good eye and a steady hand.

Now I also have problems as far as my anxiety and panic attacks. Also this would be the worst time for me because when I was at the flea market I smoked more. When I wasn't busy I would smoke because of boredom. I would do the flea market on Saturday and Sundays. It would be a very long day. In order to get a good spot I would have to be there about 5:30am and I would be there until 2pm maybe longer. So as you can see it was a long day, a long day for me to smoke. On days like this I would smoke at least three maybe four packs while I was at the market. My anxiety levels were high. Whenever someone wanted a piece of jewelry I would have to ask them to please walk around and see the different vendors while I made their necklace. My hands shook so much because of my anxiety so it made it hard for me to make the chains. I would talk to my counselor about this and both of us would try to figure out what I could do to help me thru these difficult times.

Finally The Day Comes, Yes October 6, 2001. I remember it to this very day. I had an appointment with Jim, my counselor. I didn't feel good at all, my anxiety levels was very high there was some form of a panic attack coming in. I was trying to keep my appointment; well I made it to his office. I went into him and said, "Jim this is it, I cannot take it any longer. I am going to quit smoking today." I couldn't even stay for our meeting. I did use the NeCoderm CQ patch. I used it longer then it is prescribed by the manufacture. I did it with my doctors' ok. What I did was cut them into quarters and thus cutting my dosage of the nicotine more of what was prescribed. I did this for six months. Then one day, don't remember that date but I just stopped using the patch. Till this day I remain smoke free. I owe my friend Jim Mel of Step-a Head a big thanks and the biggest thank you is to God Himself whom without Him I could not have made it.

Let me tell you sort of a funny story of how I actually got to be a non-smoker. You remember how I told you my mother passed away in July of 1999. My mother was a nag, God love her. Every time I would have a cigarette she would say, "Bruce you just had a cigarette." Or "You're smoking again?" Well she did this to God, she got on His back every day and nagged Him up there in Heaven and finally He got tired of it. He said, "Ok Helen if I give your son another miracle and make him a non-smoker will you get off my back?" She said back to Him, yes I will. Well as you can see she did get off of His back because today I am a non-smoker.

Well it sounds like a good ending to my story; however sad to say but there is not a good ending to my story. All these years I may not have emphized on how many times I was very sick with bronchitis. Then in my forties it turned into emphiama/COPD. In 2001 to 2003 I had to be on oxygen all the time 24/7 and use the nebulizer treatments at home. Today at fifty years old I am hanging in there. I have my bouts with my bronchitis. Once I get treatment for it and a little time I recover. ; However I will never get rid of my chronic cough. It is a bothersome to me.

My advice to anyone who smokes it doesn't matter how old you are, how long you have smoked for or how your health is. Stop smoking or start working on it today for your own good. Yes smoking causes a lot of deaths but my friends the worst part of this is the quality of life. When you lose the quality of life then it is like living in a prison.

No matter when you quit each year that you obstain from it you body is in the healing process so your quality of life will get better. Don't say I am young and it is not bothering me that is what I said when I first started , next thing I knew it I was addicted t it and it didn't take me long. Once you become addicted to this poison trying to quit is not easy but it is possible. Trust me I was King of the smokers I would say.

God Bless and Good luck to you

Start today

Today is the first day of the rest of your life. Live it well, live it in good health.

Cigarette-Today's Number One Killer

I did some research on my own to see just how bad cigarette smoking is to our health. The main point I intend to make by the end of this chapter is to convince anyone that the cigarette companies should be held liable by anyone who has major health problems or by the families of anyone who has died because of smoking. I myself was a smoker for twenty-five years and I know firsthand how hard it is to quit because of the withdrawal symptoms. Cigarette companies should be held liable for major health problems or deaths they cause to smokers and their families.

There are two lung diseases we know of that are caused by smoking. One is chronic bronchitis and the other is emphysema. C.O.P.D. which stands for Chronic Obstructive Pulmonary Disease is a term referring to the two lung diseases. Smoking is known to be the major cause for death of those who have C.O.P.D. It claimed the lives of 120,000 Americans in 2002. C.O.P.D. was the fourth leading cause of death. (Lungusa.org)

There is another way smoking kills. That is by lung cancer. An estimated 160,440 deaths from lung cancer will occur in the U.S. during 2004. One type of lung cancer is non-small cell lung cancer which usually spreads to different parts of the body more slowly than small cell lung cancer. The lunre are three types of non-small cell cancer. They are: squamous cell carcinoma, adenocarecinoma, and large cell carcinoma. Oat cell cancer is a small cell lung cancer it accounts for twenty percent of all lung cancer. (Lungusa.org)

Lung cancer is caused by smoking 87% of the time. A good portion of lung cancer can be prevented. There are over 4,000 different chemicals in cigarettes which are known to be cancer- causing substances or carcinogens. If you smoke cigars or pipe it will also increase your risk of getting lung cancer. (Lungusa.org)

Now is the time to stop smoking. If a person continues to smoke, the longer they smoke the higher risk they will have of getting lung cancer. However, if a person stops now, the risk of getting lung cancer will decrease each year. The normal cell will replace the abnormal cell; in fact, the longer a person a person goes smoke-free the less chance they will have of developing other smoke related diseases like chronic bronchitis, emphysema, heart disease and stroke. (Lungusa.org)

It is known that non-smokers are also affected by smoking. We call this second hand smoke. Approximately 3,000 lung cancer deaths are the result per year. ILungusa.org)

Smoking was first linked to diseases by the Surgeon General in 1964. Later on, in 2004 the Surgeon General expanded the list of diseases caused by smoking, which included abdominal aortic aneurysm, acute myeloid leukemia, cataracts, cervical cancer, kidney cancer, pancreatic cancer, pneumonia, periodontitis, and stomach cancer. These diseases are added to those that are already known to be caused by cigarette smoking. (cdc.gov).

Smoking cost the government and private health insurance companies a lot of unnecessary money. The reason I say unnecessary is because these illnesses or diseases are all preventable by not smoking. (Cdc.gov). Also, the smokers are sick more than non smokers; therefore, they are more likely to be absent from work. According to the Surgeon General's report a smoker has a lower rate after surgery compared to a non-smoker. This is because the smoker could develop postoperative pneumonia or other respiratory complications. Also smoking can cause periodontitis. This is a serious gum disease that can lead to loss of teeth and bone tissue. (cdc.gov). Let me add to this. In was in a car accident in 1998 and I had to have back surgery. I was not able to have it done, because after I was anesthetized I was laid on my stomach and then quickly I went into respiratory distress. The next thing I recall I was being rushed to I.C.U. unit of the hospital and I was on the ventilator. I had no idea what was going on. I could not talk of course but I tried to ask if the doctor was able to do the surgery, I was told no. The doctor told me that I had stopped breathing before they were able to start the surgery. This was due to the condition my lungs were in. I was on the ventilator and in the I.C.U. unit for three to four days, but finally I was taken off if to see if I was able to breathe on my own. . It was hard when they took the tube out of my throat; however I was able to breathe. After I was in I.C.U. they transferred me to a regular room. I had to be on oxygen and even once I was discharged the doctor still had me on oxygen 24/7. A few months later, after being on medications and breathing treatments, the doctors attempted surgery once again. This time they were able to do the surgery, but I did have to be on the ventilator again. I went through the surgery ok. After this I was still on oxygen mostly at bed time and during the day if I needed it. You would think after almost dying I would quit smoking well the sad news is I did not quit.

I did not identify my illness as being due to smoking until years later, when I finally did quit, and after some time I had regained my health. Now today being a non-smoker I feel much better. I still have health problems due to the smoking, but they are not nearly as bad as they were back then. It was a long though road as I gave up the cigarettes. I tied countless times, not succeeding and I never thought I would be able to give them up. People do not realize what nicotine does to a person.

I continued to smoke until finally in 2001 I had my last cigarette. I moved up to N.J. in 2000 and my lung condition followed me. I would get very light headed and feeling like I was going to pass out. This forced me to quit. The doctor I was seeing at the time had someone from the hospital come out to my house and put me on the oxygen meter. I walked for about fifteen minutes outside my house. As I walked the lower my oxygen level dropped. It fell under 86% which qualifies me to be put on oxygen by Medicare. So this just started another hard road to be on. I was delivering newspapers at this time. Having to be on oxygen did not stop me. I had small O2 bottles stocked up at my house. No matter where I went I had to lug those bottles. Pending on how long I was going to be out how many bottles I would have to take. Yes by this time I did not smoke but it still haunted me. In November of 2003 finally I was able to be taken off the oxygen. Up to this day I still have to be on it; however only at bedtime. My lungs have improved over the years of not smoking; but once again I still have my bouts of Chronic Bronchitis.

You may say well if you still get sick why you stopped smoking. I have to say if I continued to smoke in 2001 I really do not think I will be here and

A lot of young people today are smoking cigarettes. Due to the nicotine in cigarettes, they find it hard to quit. It is the same way in adults, because nicotine in cigarett4es makes it difficult for someone to quit smoking. (drugabuse.gov)

I have mentioned that smoking is harmful. Here is just another way smoking causes health problems for women who are pregnant and smoke. There can be such complications as premature birth, low birth weight infants, still birth, and infant death. This leading cause of infant death is low birth weight from which more than 300,000 deaths annually result. There are so many complications that can result during pregnancy for those women who continue to smoke. (cdc.gov)

Nicotine is found I in all cigarettes and it is the substance which creates mild intoxication. When a person smokes a cigarette or tobacco product with the nicotine in it, they become addicted because they suffer from the withdrawal symptoms. These include; tension, restlessness, depression, irritability, craving for tobacco and sleep disorders. Once a person has a cigarette or gets their fix they are ok, and this is where the addiction comes into play. (Newdirectionsprogram). Nicotine is a very addictive drug and it is found to be the most widely used drug in the United States. It is even attracting the younger population, children as young as twelve if not younger are becoming addicted to cigarettes. Nicotine stimulates the central nervous system and other endocrine glands. This causes a release of glucose, but this stimulation is followed by fatigue and depression until the person has their next cigarette. This leads the abuser to seek more nicotine. A study found that when heavy smokers stopped smoking for twenty-four hours, they had increased levels of anger, hostility and aggression. (nida.nih.gov)

Today there are many ways to help people to quit smoking. My theory is there are two addictions going on in a smoker, and I experienced this myself. One addiction is the physical addiction since once the smoker has a taste of nicotine and it enters the body, they become addicted to it. They have to get their fix depending on how much they smoke, and how often they will need their quick fix. I myself smoked three to four packs a day just before I quit, so I needed a lot of nicotine. To take the place of nicotine there is the patch, gum, spray, inhalers. All of these substitutes deliver the nicotine to the body, thus taking care of the physical addiction. Then there is the second part of the addiction whish is the psychological part. This is where the addict needs support just like any other addict. I myself used the nicotine patch for six months, and also went to a counselor who specialized in nicotine addictions. I went once a week for a while, and by the grace of God I finally, with many thousand attempts of try to quit smoking, became a nonsmoker. Let me say to you just as long you have the will to want to quit and try like myself thousands of times you will eventually be a winner. On the other hand sadly to say if you do not try and give up on trying you are not a winner any longer. I say to those you have lost the battle and are a loser. I don't mean to put it like this; however it is so true.

We know if a person quits smoking their benefits will be great, and the longer they go without smoking, the greater the benefit. The American Lung Association claims that within the first twenty minutes of smoking the last cigarette, the blood pressure and pulse rate drop to normal, and the body temperature becomes normal. Within the first twenty-four hours a person's chance of a heart attack decreases; furthermore, within the first forty-eight hours nerve endings regrow and the ability of the senses like the ability to taste and smell is enhanced. As a person continues to be smoke-free, more rewards come to them: nicotine leaves the body after forty-eight to seventy-two hours, breathing is made easier, circulation improves, lung function increases, fatigue and shortness of breath decreases. The lung begin to clean and the cilia regrows. (Newdirectionsprogram.com)

I experienced the effects smoking has on a person first hand. I started smoking when I was eighteen. I developed lung problems quickly after I started to smoke, and I would get bronchitits every winter. At first I started to smoke a pack a day then, as time went on I increased the amount I smoke. I would try to quit smoking all the time, but I failed because of the nicotine that is in a cigarette. I got very sick when I was in my early thirties. At first I was being treated mediclly and had a test done, which resulted in arsenic in my system. At that time doctors were not aware of what was in cigarettes, especially not arsenic. I was in the hospital at the time, and I had a test done two weeks after, however, there was no arsenic in my system. This is because I was in the hospital and only smoked eight cigarettes a day. After a while, even though I was being treated medically, I was not getting any help. Finally I had to do something, because I felt very bad; so bad that I needed to be in the hospital, so I started the long road with many different stays in the psychological hospitals. I would go in feeling very bad, I would be in for about two weeks at a time, and again only be able to smoke eight cigarettes a day so by the end of my stay I would be feeling better. Then I would go back to smoking two to three packs a day, and I would start to feel all burnt out again.

My feelings are the cigarette companies should be held liable because of the nicotine found in cigarettes. Yes a person chooses at first to pick up the cigarette, but it is that first cigarette, that first introduction to cigarettes. I remember my first cigarette, and I became addicted almost instantly. Also, there are so many chemicals involved which cause illness and even leads to death. The cigarette companies are literally getting away with murder. I feel the reason why cigarette companies are getting away with this is because there is a lot of money being made. There are a lot of illness which are related to smoking, therefore the cigarette companies are at fault. They should finally start paying for the unknown number of people who have died because of smoking, and even now are ill. Today we are finding out that even people who don't smoke, and are around smoke can pay a price. They are suspectible to cigarette smoke related illness, just as the smoker. Why should they pay a price of good health or maybe even their life? Perhaps if the government cracks down on the cigarettes companies and make them liable for their wrong doings, maybe manufacturers would cut down the nicotine in cigarettes, making them less addictive. Therefore we would not see many people, who would find it hard to quit smoking, should they chose to quit. I hear that today, younger people who have just started to smoke are getting sick, and want to quit but, say it is hard and they cannot. The answer is because of the nicotine in the cigarette. Even though we have made it law that you have to be twenty-one to smoke there are kids much younger who are smoking today. I think there are younger kids smoking today than when I was their age. Again, we are not cracking down on the cigarette companies enough. If they would start to have to pay money, it may give them an incentive to do something. Yes, I have seen some commercials of TV. from some cigarette companies that advise smokers how to quit, but I still feel they are not doing enough (cdc.gov).

I know there is more research against cigarettes. I have only put a dent in the subject of the number one killer in my opinion... We need to act today before smoking continues to kill tomorrow.

Changes that will happen the longer you are a non-smoker

Time Since Quit	Effects on Your Body
• 20 minutes	Blood Pressure and pulse will return to normal Cirulation in your hands and feet will get better
• 8 hours	the oxygen in your blood goes to a normal level Your level of carbon Returns to normal
• 1 day	the chance of you dying of A heart attack decreases
• 2 to 3 days	your senses will improve
• 2 to 12 weeks	Blood flow, breathing and Walking gets better

- 1 to 9 months   your lungs and sinus gets
  Better
  Less coughing, shortness of
  breath and chance of infections
  you will find

- 1 year   the risk of heart diseases lessens to half of a smoker

- 5years   Your chance of lung cancer decrease. Many other cancers related diseases decrease. Such as: mouth, pancreas, kidney, bladder, esophagus and mouth and throat cancer.

- 10   Risk of lung cancer is cut in half

- 15 years   Your risk of having heart disease Is just as low as that of a person who never smoked.
  (Quit-Now)

Free at last, Free at last, Thank God I'm free at last.

(Martin Luther King)

Why is it hard to quit smoking?

The definition of addiction according to Dictionary.com

The state of being enslaved to a habit or practice or to something that is psychologically or physicallyhabit-forming, as narcotics, to such an extent that its cessation causes severe trauma.

The definition of habit forming according to Dictionary.com.

Tending to cause or encourage addiction, especially through physiological dependence: *habit-forming drugs*

The tobacco companies put nicotine in the cigarettes so you do get addicted so you want and buy more cigarettes. The government should be stricter on allowing this to happen. Cigarettes should be more controlled by how much nicotine is put in them. The FDA should do their job and make this happen. Also I feel people that have serious illness from smoking or even the families of a smoker which has died to smoking should be able to make the cigarette companies held liable. We sue drug companies today for many different side effects they have on a person so what is different about the cigarette. I tell you the government makes so much money on the taxes of them and they don't lose it. The judges disregard this issue also. Perhaps everyone involved should reevaluate this and allow the smoker or family to make the companies liable hitting them hard and sue. Thus perhaps if this happens the cigarette companies will make cigarettes not t be so addicting. They won't due this unless we force them to. So big government and FDA do your job. Stop allowing this to happen. I advice anyone that has this addiction to call your congressman, senator even write the FDA how you feel. This must stop and it will if we make it happen.

There are three different addictions that are happen when you quit smoking.

> One is there is an emotional addiction. This is how you feel when you smoke. Your belief about smoking cigarettes.   Last what you actually think about the use tobacco use.

> Second is the behavioral addiction. This is how you respond to the places and times you want to smoke. Such as after you wake up in the morning, lunch and super times. This is the time most addicts have the craving for a cigarette. This can be both behavioral and physical addiction going on in your mind and system.

> The third is when your body is use to having nicotine and requires more due to the effects

nicotine has on the system. This can and is the reason why smokers have such a hard time to give up the cigarettes.

This is the viscous cycle nicotine has your body and mind. First you light that first cigarette of the day. Once you breathe in that cigarette the nicotine travels to the brain very quickly. It takes just seven seconds with each puff you take. Then after that first cigarette you feel by relaxed and calm. Then a nicotine level in your body quickly falls after a cigarette. You start to feel a craving for another smoke. When this happens you say to yourself, "I need another cigarette. You start to feel irritable and restless until you satisfy the craving and put more nicotine in your system. Yes I mean picking up that cancer stick and putting it in your mouth.

Ways to Quit Smoking

Just in case you say to yourself I am not going to be able to quit smoking. Well you are wrong. I never thought I would be a non smoker today but because I did not give up on trying quitting and finally won the battle. As I have said in previous chapter you health will improve each day that you don't smoke.

1. First you have to make the decision that you want to quit. Make a promise to yourself that you will succeed stopping your smoking habit. You may have mixed feelings from time to time; however realize this is ok. When you say to yourself you don't want to quit stick to not smoking.
2. Think of the reasons you want to quit.
    a. Your health will improve and live a longer life.
    b. The money you will save not having to buy cigarettes. With the cost of cigarettes today who can afford them.
    c. You will have more time for yourself from not taking that smoke break. You may not realize the time you waste while you are smoking

d. Think about the time you spend on going out and buying the cigarettes
   e. The panic one has when either totally out of cigarettes or down to the last few.
   f. Not being short of breath or coughing as much
   g. Set a better example for the younger generation.
3. Think for a while and write down the reasons you want to quit smoking
4. Remember the urge to smoke will still be with you; however this will come and go. The more you say no to smoking the more you will not want to smoke.
5. Tips on getting thru that urge to smoke.
   a. Keep other things around you instead of your cigarettes. Good examples are carrots, pickles, sunflower seeds, apples, celery, raisins, sugar free gum and whatever else you like that is good for you.
   b. Take a shower when that urge comes. Wash your hands or clean the dishes in other words keep yourself busy when you want a cigarette very badly.

6. Relax
    a. Take 10 slow, deep breaths and hold the last one.
    b. Then breathe out slowly
    c. Relax your muscles.
    d. Picture yourself in a soothing, pleasant scene.
    e. Just take a break from it all for a moment.
    f. Think only of peaceful image and nothing else.
7. Light a candle or incense instead of a cigarette.
8. Stay out of areas where people are smoking. Do not be around cigarettes at all.
9. Remember this is just like drinking. When one is an alcoholic that person cannot pickup just one drink so it is the same with smoking. You cannot pickup one cigarette.
10. As we know smoking is a habit, addiction. There are good habits and addictions for you; it is just a matter of finding one. Just a few good suggestions.
    a. Find a support group for nicotine addictions. If there are non in your area attend another support group for addictions.
    b. Seek counseling

    c. If you do not attend church regularly start now. That is a very good addiction to pick up. The reason why I call it an addiction is mainly because once you get use to attending church on a regular basis is becomes a habit and a normal routine. What a better way to find help to quit all addictions is going right to the top and that is your higher power no matter which you see it to be.

11. Keep active in the spring and summer you can go swimming, jogging, play tennis, bike riding or even shoot baskets. How can you smoke while doing any of these activies? The answer is you can't. If you have dogs take him or her for walk.
12. Keep your hand busy because they are use to the habit of picking up a cigarette. If you like crossword puzzles, needle work, painting, wood working, gardening or even doing the normal house hold chores. All of these will surely keep your mind off of smoking along with keeping yourself busy.
13. Each day that goes by not smoking you will find your taste for foods will get better. I would suggest you to brush your teeth and use mouth wash frequently.

The body begins to heal within 20 minutes after you have had your last cigarette. The nicotine and poison start to leave your body. Your oxygen level in your blood rises to the normal level. The pulse rate also goes back to normal.

- Your taste and senses are better
- You will be able to breathe easier
- Your smokers "hack" will start to go away. You will find that annoying cough will be with you for a while.

Within a few days of being smoke free you will be amazed on other things you will notice. Hang in there you are taking the right step. That is reading this book means you want to do something about your habit. This will not happen overnight. It is a battle but you are a winner and you can and will do it. Keep saying that to yourself. I am a non-smoker, I am smoke free, and I do not buy cigarettes any longer. The thing I am trying to point out is keep positive thoughts in your mind especially when that tough time comes and you want to pick up cigarettes.

Let me share just one scripture out of the Bible that help me get over my addictions. It is Matthew 10:1 when they inquired of Jesus why they were not able to drive the demon out, the Master replied, "Because you have so little faith. I tell you the truth, if you have faith as small as a mustard seed, you can say to this mountain, 'move from here to there' and it will move; nothing we are impossible for you". So what I am saying to you is start off with just a little faith and believe that you will be a non-smoker. The longer you practice this the stronger your faith will be. So therefore you will be a non-smoker. Just believe! Have the tiniest amount of faith. You are a winner. Keep say that to yourself.

After being tobaccos free for three days the nicotine will leave your body. As this goes on the body starts to repair itself. In the beginning you will feel worse instead of better but don't let that scare you. The withdrawal feelings can be hard. They are a sign that your body is in the healing process. You are on your way to freedom. Keep up the good work.

The long-term rewards of being a non-smoker

You will live longer. More than 450,000 deaths each year are contributed to tobacco use. Of those deaths at least 170,000 are from cancer.

You will find each day you are tobacco free you are adding more days to your life. You will be healthier.

You will lower the risk of death from the following disease:

- Lung cancer
- Heart disease
- Stroke
- Chronic bronchitis
- Emphysema
- And more types of cancer

Also you are now thinking of your loved ones. As I have mentioned about second hand smoke with you being a non-smoker you are adding years to those around you. Should they be family, friends, co-workers or just the general public. This will lead you to a happier and healthier life. Isn't this great. If you are young and a smoker right now just think once you quit the longer you will live and the less you will suffer. Trust me the quality of your life will come back. The key thing for anyone no matter what your age is quit today, set a start date and stick to it. You will be setting a good example to anyone that smokes. You can be a good role model even if you are young perhaps once you get through the hard days you may be able to help your friend. Also think of this buddy up with someone else that my want to quit.

Withdrawal

The symptoms you may or may not feel.

- Depressed
- Not able to sleep
- Cranky, frustrated, anger
- Anxiety, nervous, restless
- Difficult concentrating
- Increase in appetite
- Weight gain

Everyone is different, some may have all of the above and some may have a few. Also the intensity is different with everyone. Some may be server and for a longer time and others may be the opposite.

Some of the following medications may help you get thru the physical part of the addictions. What most of them do is instead of getting the nicotine in your system by the cigarette they give you nicotine in the forms the medication. Such as:

- Nicotine gum
- Nicotine inhaler
- Nicotine lozenge
- Nicotine nasal spray
- Nicotine patch

- Bupropion SR pills
- Varencine pills

Best thing to do I would advise is check with your medical doctor because they are coming out with something new every day. Remember this is just like any other medication. Some of them will help others where some may not. Also the side effects for everyone are different. I would advise you if you so have any side effect tell your doctor. He will be able to determine whether you should continue on the medication or not. It is very important that you keep in touch with all your doctors you see should they be your medical doctor or you phsyicirtist.

I say for me the first two weeks was the hardest. I found that the symptoms of withdrawal were the strongest. For me thanks to the patch I was still able to get the nicotine I need in my body thus get through those tough days. By all means if you are using any of these products do not have a cigarette at all. This can just cause some very serious complications.

I want to express my sincere luck to you during your hard road of this battle. Remember I am a winner. You read this book to see what you can do to become a non-smoker. That is half the battle. You are on the road to freedom. Congratulations.

Next Step

Ok after all of that information you should be ready to quit. Now you know how bad smoking is to your health and I think you would like to live a longer and healthier life.

You will know when it is time to quit. It is time to choose a quit date. Tell your friends, family or co-workers what your goal it and a date that you have set. I have to let you know that this is not an easy journey but you can do it. No matter how many times you try and fail don't give up. If you don't give up one day you can say to yourself the battle is over and I am a winner. As I have mentioned earlier use the medications that will help you. Some people and quit cold turkey that's great each person is different. Don't feel like you are a weak person by not being able to just quit. God gives us many tools to get over things in our lives. Just one example for those whom are diabetics there is many different medications to battle this and live a healthier life. So the same thing here, God give us aids to help us battle the becoming a non-smoker. One thing you will notice is an urge to eat more. Is that bad? No, all you have to do it eat the right foods. If you are a burger feen just find a healthier food that you like and replace it with that. Drink plenty of fluids; this will wash your system out. Also a good idea is exercise. This will help you in many ways that I do not think you realize it. First by exersing this will help you the control of weight gain. Also you will be reliving the stress that comes with the beginning of your battle. Exercising balances out the chemicals in our brain. So if you exercise, eat the correct meals it is just a win, win switchuation. I would recommend you make this a part of your life even after you quit.

Get yourself ready to quit. 2 weeks before your quit date you should find the things that you like to do without smoking and does not allow smoking. Start being active, exercise at least three times a week. Make sure you talk to your doctor before starting any type of exercise. You want to make sure you are in good health. Start looking into ways you can cope during that time of the urge to smoke.

A week before your quit date stop smoking in both your home and car. Do not let anyone smoke in them. Start working on quitting. Stretch out the time you smoke. Such as have a cigarette every two hours. Think of ways to change your daily routine. Get up later if you do not have to get up. Drink tea instead of coffee and by all means start to walk.

Picking a quit date for every one may differ. Some people may want to quit during the work week. This is a good idea for several reasons. First I think you know that you are busy and cannot smoke as much you would normally do if you were just hanging around doing nothing. A lot of people that chose this start it off by picking a Monday morning as their quit date. Although some may find the weekend is better for them. They find there is less stress than during the work week. You can plan some places which you can not smoke at, such as gong to the movies. This will be beneficial for a lot of other reasons than just to help you not smoke. Right off the bat watching a movie is entertainment. It gets your mind off of everything, stress, pressure and getting your mind off having a smoke. You can find other smoke free places you like to go to. I cannot insist enough keep yourself busy. If you have a family member or friend whom smokes perhaps they can join you in your battle to freedom. You can help each other out. Call each other when the urge to smoke comes on. Usually the craving last for about five minutes. So if you can find something to get your mind it then you will not want to have those cigarettes. The more you practice this the longer you will go time wise without that smoke. For me the first two weeks was the hardest. Each week that went by just got easier and easier. If you can get thru this you also will find it getting easier. Next thing you will know a month as gone by being smoke free. Wow you are on the road being a non-smoker. Reward yourself for each milestone. Such as each month that goes by being smoke free treat yourself to something you like or like to do. Tell everyone you know of your accomplishments. Like each month that has gone by say wow I can't believe it has been x amount of time I have not smoked. I myself do this every once in a while even though it has been over ten years since I quit. Manly I do this so those that come across my path and are smokers may realize this becoming a non-smoker is possible. My goal is hopefully they follow my short story and also in time become a non-smoker. You may have to read this book more than one time. Each time you read it you will get something different out of it. Reading is another good pass time to help you get thru the hard days. Pick a book which you like to read also a subject you are interested in. What I am saying to you is keep your mind on other things and keep it busy. Get a calendar where you will see it all the time such as your refrigerator. As each day that goes by just put a big X on that day. Next thing you will see it has been a whole week, then two weeks etc. You are on the road to becoming a non-smoker. Remember you can do it. Just find the thing that is best for you. I have given many different ways and how I became a non-smoker. Everyone is different I say many times.

Ok you have made it this far. Now you are the night before your quit date. Get together anything at pertains to smoking. Throw away whatever cigarettes you have, go one step further with this. Put all of your cigarettes in your sink and pour water over them. They are now ready to throw out. Get anything else such as any lighters or ashtrays you have around the house. Go into your car and wash the ash tray in it. If you can take it for a wash and have a clean sent sprayed in it. If you cannot take it to the car wash get some type of disinfect spray you like and spray it inside. Do this every day, eventually the odder will fade away. If you plan on using any type of medications mentioned in this book read up on it and review the correct ways to use it. Practice the ways that will get you through the urge. You want to remember ways to handle the stress which comes along being smoke free. Use deep breathing exercises and whatever other ways you have decided will aid you through these hard days. Talk, talk, talk when you are feeling stressed out find anyone to talk to it may be your best friend, family member, pastor/priest or a therapist. Anyone you feel comfortable with. The key thing here is not to hold the stress that comes along with being without a cigarette as time goes by.

When the Urge to Smoke Happens

You will find the urge to smoke a lot in the beginning, this is normal. The longer you say no to the cigarette the less the urges will happen. What happens is in the beginning your body still craves the nicotine. There are those triggers or habits such as at all meal times. I think everyone that smokes loves that cigarette after a good meal. Some people feel the urge to have a smoke while they are talking on the phone or having a cup of coffee. You will find these urges will be tough especially in the first two to three weeks after quitting. It is very important you have a plan in place to get you thru the urge. The key think is remember the urge for that cigarette will only be with you for about five or ten minutes, get through that. The more you do it the longer apart the urge will come on you. After you get through the critical time which is usually two to three weeks your on the road to freedom. Wow you don't believe it you are doing real well. You are still reading this book and that is the first important step. There may be times you slip up and that is ok. The main thing is just get back on track of not smoking

Why do you want to quit?

Think of what tobacco is to you. When I finally quit I went through a grieving process. I called the cigarettes my best friend even now I know it wasn't. It actually was my worst enemy. Once I did not have that pack of cigarettes in my pocket I felt as though someone has left me. You may ask how I got over this. Actually I had to go thru the grieving process as though someone has died. I worked with a very good addiction counselor. I saw this person once a week for almost six months. I went to him and talked about how my week was. I would tell him the problems and symptoms I was battling without both the nicotine and the cigarette. This made it easier for me. I think this would be a very good suggestion for you also. There are a lot of places today which works on a sliding scale according to your income. The thing here is to find that organization or counselor that provides their services on a sliding scale. At the end of this book I will give you many resources including the counselor whom helped me. He may not be in your area or state; however perhaps he can guide to find a place for you to start off with. Do everything you can and utilized every resource you find. Don't do this alone.

Know Your Coping Skills

You want to be prepared for when those sudden urges comes to you. There are things that you can do to get over that hard few minutes. As I maybe have mentioned earlier your urge to smoke will just last a very short time. Now what can you do when those urges happen. Well there are a lot of things that you can do.

Below are just a few samples:

- Take a walk
- Do house work
- Brush your teeth after each meal
- Treat yourself to a cup of coffee, tea, mint or candy
- Spend some time with your dog. Take him or her for a walk
- If you do not have a dog then spend time with whatever pet you have.
- Drink your coffee or tea at a different place
- Keep your hands busy by writing or drawing. Anything you do that keeps your hands busy.

A Few Ways to Practice Quitting

By following these examples can make quitting easier and it increase your success. Pick a time that you are not going to have a cigarette. Replace that time with a positive activity. Don't smoke the first two hours you are awake. Try not to smoke after meals. Do something else during that time. Keep yourself busy during these times. This is the most important thing you need to do to be successful. As time goes by and you are ready for the next step pick another time during the day. Don't smoke for a whole hour. Then as you get thru this time add another hour. If you keep on doing this you will find that you made the biggest important step. Now you are a non-smoker.

How to Cope with Stress

I have to tell you the truth during the hard time of not smoking your stress level will rise. The thing is know how to control the stress. When stress comes in you will find it hard to think clearly and you will feel more nervous. Of course we all have stress from time to time; but it is how we cope with the stress.

Below are a few ideas you can practice whenever you feel stress:

- Deep breathing
- Be sure you get enough sleep
- Take a walk
- Pray or meditate
- Eat healthy
- Take time out take a nap
- Talk to a friend
- Watch a movie

The above are just a few suggestions you can practice when you feel stress full. I cannot express how it is important you keep busy.

Pick Some People that Can Help You during this Time

Don't try to do this on your own. Find people that you can trust and feel comfortable talking to. They can be a member of your family, co-workers or friends. If you know of someone that has already quit this is great. They will be able to help you along the hard road of being a non-smoker. Do not pick someone who is still smoking. These people will help you by listening when you need to talk. They will cheer you up and not be judgmental. They will help you by keeping contact with you. Let them help you however they want. This is another important part of getting thru the hard days.

Clean up Your Environment

It's time to get rid of that stinky smell of tobacco. This is just another step towards freedom. Clean all of the areas you will be in.

Such as:

- Your home, clean all of the rooms you go in
- Get rid of all of the ash trays you have
- Clean your car good
- Get rid of all cigarettes you have left

The urge to have a cigarette is stronger if you have any around. You will find it being easier to quit if you do not have any tobacco products around.

What can you do if you have friends which smoke?

The first thing you would want to do with your friends that do smoke is tell them what you are doing. Let them know you are going to quit. Tell them the day and date you are going to start. Ask them if they can smoke away from you. It may be hard if you are either over their house or in their car. This is your decision on how you handle this. If they smoke it their house more than likely if they are good friends they will go out of the house for this time. If they smoke in their house then what I will do it politely go outside while they are smoking. Then what can you do if you are in their car. I would ask them if they can wait to have a cigarette and have the cigarette out of the car. I will say this again if they are a true friend they will understand and not smoke in their car.

You have to remember it is you that is in control. There are things that you can do to help staying friends with those that do smoke. If you are all together no matter what you all are doing and they do light up a cigarette what can you do to distract yourself from joining them and have a smoke? Find something you like to do such as chew on a stray, put a puzzle together or whatever you can do that you like.

Some people put sticky notes all around. They put them in all of the rooms of their house and also their car. This is helpful to remind you that you are a non-smoker.

Use Medications that Makes Quitting Smoking Easier

There are many different medications that aid you to become a non-smoker. I may have mentioned this earlier but it is very important to use any tool that will help you become a non-smoker. There are some people that can just stop and not have another cigarette. This is great for them however this may not be you. I myself had to use the patch. Without the patch I do not think I would have stop smoking. Talk to your medical doctor and see what he recommends. He knows what medications you are on presently and determine what will be best for you. Remember everyone is different, just because one aid does not work on another person does not mean it will not help you. You will not know it until you try the medication. Also another thing to keep in mind is to use the medication the way you are supposing to. I know of some people which will put the patch on and take if off to have a cigarette. This can be very dangerous. What people do not realize is any of these aids you are still getting nicotine in your system. By using these aids and having a smoke increases your chances of having a heart attack and more. So do not use both the nicotine aid and your cigarette.

What Medications can Help You Quit?

Today we have many ways to help us quit smoking. We know that in cigarettes there are not only a lot of poisons but also nicotine. Nicotine is very addicted and this is why it is so hard to quit smoking. All of the nicotine medication is good to use. This is depending on the person. What happens when a person use any of these products they are given nicotine only. They do not breathe in the deadly smoke that cigarettes put out. I know some of you may be thinking well if you use these it is just a replacement for the cigarette. This is not correct; again I say that these medications wean people from nicotine. They do this by lowering the mg as time goes by. This makes the person less dependent on the cigarettes. Eventually the person is able to quit. Now let me tell you my experience with this. Almost all of my life I tried to quit many times. One of the ways I used was the Nicotine Patch. This would work for a few weeks or more but I slipped up and gave in. I would try to quit again and again. Finally by not giving up and using the patch I was able to quit. What I am saying to you is no matter what the quit smoking aid you use don't give up if you fall one time or another. As I mentioned I used the patch many times and gave in after using it for a few weeks but I just continued with it. Because I never gave up on using the patch system I can now say to you that I have been smoke free since October 6, 2001. The patch is easy to use. All you have to do is find a place on your body to put it on. You should always put the patch above your waist but below your neck. Change the places you put the patch on every day. Once you use it you will find it is easy to use. It will give you a steady dose of nicotine throughout the day. You can find patches at many different drug stores and no prescription is needed. The funny thing is you will find by doing this you will save a lot of money each day. Also your health will start to improve immediately

There are other medications there are out there than can help you also. I am listing them below. Some of them can be used as a combination. Check with your doctor the correct way to use all nicotine products. Be sure to check with him if you have any health conditions before you take any of these. Also there are many other ways you can try. Remember what I say just because it did not work for someone else does not mean it will work for you. I say to you just try until you know it is not for you.

Other medications to try:
- Nicotine Lozenges
- Nicotine Inhaler
- Nicotine Inhaler
- Nicotine Nasal Spray
- Bupropion SR
  (Also known as Zyban or Wellbutin)
- Varenicline (Also known as Chantix)

Check with Your Doctor before Trying the Following:
- Combined Nicotine Patch and Gum
- Combined Nicotine Patch and Lozenges

Become a nonsmoker don't be just a quitter. You will find the first two weeks are the hardest this was my hardest time. After that it is all downhill. Don't get me wrong you will still have some tough days ahead of you but the more you say no to that urge you have the more days are going to go by as a nonsmoker. The next thing you will know is you are a nonsmoker. The key to get you thru those urges is plan ahead of time and know what you are going to do. You can go for a walk, chew something you like, keep busy. The next thing you will know it the time went by so fast that urge is over. You and people around you have to realize that you may feel grouchy, nervous and stressed. This is normal; your body is still craving nicotine. You have to adjust your life without cigarettes. I do have good news for you it does get easier as time goes by and the longer you are with that cigarette. Use whatever you have until you know you are thru the craving for nicotine. Sometime you will have to use the product i.e. Nicotine patch longer that it tells you. Do not do this until you check with your doctor. It is important thru out this you keep in touch with him or her. If you are experiencing any side effects call him or her. Trust me when I say this, I know it first hand, the rewards being a nonsmoker are great. I listed them earlier in this book.

Here are some tips that may help you during the first two weeks without that cigarette. Stay away from other smokers if you can. Stay away from areas that are for smokers. Of course do not smoke, not even one puff. Talk to your doctor so you both can decide which medication is right for you. Get rid of all cigarettes and ashtrays. This is very important, do not have anything in your house or car that is smoking related. Use all of your coping skills you have learned. Be sure you have people that will support you during this hard time in your life. If you find that you need get yourself a counselor. Another good idea is find out where the nearest Nicotine Anonymous meetings are. If you attend these meetings see if there is a sponsor whom will help you. When I quit I made a list of reasons for quitting and posted it on the refrigerator where I would see it all the time I went in to it. Celebrate each week you are smoke free. Just think of the money you have saved by not buying any smokes. Use this money to take yourself out or any type of reward you would like. If you drink alcohol try to stay away from it. If you find it hard not to drink do it moderately. For me whenever I drank I would smoke and smoke even more. However; you do want to quit two things at one time. At this time the important thing for you is not to have a cigarette.

When that urge comes to you take deep breaths and by all means stay active.

With the high cost of cigarettes today you will be saving a lot of money. When your urge comes to you just think of how much money you are saving on that day and go further; that week, month and the whole year. This will make you realize how much money is being wasted. Also by now you must have some type of health related problems. A lot of people this means they miss some days from work. This means lots of income so that ads to the cost of that cancer stick and you don't even realize this.

  Things you can do when the withdrawal symptoms hit

Find something that will substitute that will replace the cigarette. You might find using a tooth pick or doing a cross word puzzle. This will get your mind off of having a cigarette. Other ways could be by drinking water or practice taking deep breaths. You will find most urges goes away within five minutes. So if you can find something positive you can do for just 5 minutes you will get thru the urge. If you are using any of the nicotine replacement products this is the time you need them the most. Be sure you are using them the way they are prescribed to you.

What withdrawal symptoms can you expect?

You will find a strong urge for a cigarette. This is normal because your body is craving the nicotine which comes in the cigarette. Keep you self busy during the time. If you are using any nicotine aids before you are properly using it at this time.

Another symptom to expect you may feel very tired during the day. This should last for about two weeks. When you feel this way it's time to take a walk or do some type of activity. Again I cannot urge you how important it is to keep yourself busy.

You can feel restless, as if you have too much energy and cannot sit still. If you are drinking a lot of products which has caffeine it them such as: soda, coffee, tea try cutting back on them as much as you can. This will just add to your restlessness.

Another symptom you may experience is trouble sleeping. The way you can battle this is exercise. You will find doing this can help improve your sleep. As we know excising can make you tired.

Out of all of the symptoms other than the craving for nicotine I wanted something to eat. I would just eat and I would eat too much. I would eat a lot of stuff I was not supposed to have like sweets. Of course I gained a lot of weight. If you follow what I did you also will gain weight. This is controllable but this also will not be easy. You can eat a lot but eat the right food. When you see that cake you want think of something that is good for you. Choose foods that are filling but are low in fat and sugar.

There are other withdrawal symptoms you can expect. Should you have any symptom which you do not usually have consult your doctor. He is the best person to tell being he or she knows you and your medical history.

Now that you are a Non-Smoker

Congratulations you have made it now it's time for you to continue being a non-smoker. Remember do not smoke at all not even one puff. That one puff will just lead to another and another the next thing you know you are again being smoker. Make being a non-smoker your number one goal. You made it this far you can achieve your goal. Keep using any aids you are using. Don't think just because you have not smoked in a while that you can stop taking whatever is working for you. This is including any of the medications such as nicotine patches, gum etc... If you are going to a counselor or support group continue going to them. Also if you are going to a Nicotine Anomyus meeting and have a sponsor don't stop. Some people need to go to these meetings for the rest of their lives. It this is you it is ok. Sometime the non-smoker themselves do not need these groups but what they share in the meetings helps others. Keep that in mind. Continue staying away from those who do smoke. If they your friends they will realize how important it is for you to stay away from smoke. Use whatever copping skills you have learned. Limit your use of alcohol. I remember when I use to drink I would smoke more. If you do drink just be careful. Stay away from those high-risk situations. They are the places or people that may give you an urge to smoke. If you tried this before, quit smoking, remember what you did and why did you start back up. Learn from these past experiences. I cannot remember how many times I tried to quit the key thing was I did not give up. If I remember correctly I started trying to quit smoking I was 25 years old and when I finally did win the battle about 45 years old. You can see how long it took me to quit this does not mean it will take you just as long, everyone is different. I know of some people quit cold turkey. Then I know of some people took them just a matter of months. Please don't feel if you haven't quit on the first, second, third etc., try if you continue trying you will eventually succeeds. I am a good example. I continued trying many years finally I became a non-smoker. Today being from that nasty addiction I don't miss it at all. The first few years I did have some cravings however as you can hear I overcame them. So if you also have these cravings just continue not smoking.

Four Kinds of Risky Thinking

It is normal for you to have risky thoughts which could lead you back to smoking. It is how you deal with those thoughts that can either help you or just the opposite, hurt you. You may have a thought of remembering when you use to smoke. Just put a positive thought in place to that. Think of how you feel now verse the way you use to feel. Think of what the quality of life you are leading and going to continue to lead. I know if I did not quit when I did I honestly do not think I would be writing this book today. I really don't think I would be here either. There may be pressures of life that may hit you, such as unexpected problems. This was my down fall. I can remember when my father unexpectly pass away. I was in my third week of not having any cigarettes. After I was told he had died I went right away to a neighbor and asked for a smoke. So realize yes problems do hit us every day it is just how we deal with them. The thing to think of is look at how far you have come at that point. Think of how hard it was for you to quit at that time and if you started back smoking you would have to start all over again. As I mentioned earlier it is not ok for you to have just one cigarette or one every now and then. This will just get you back into that nasty habit. You may think that it would better if you still smoke than gain weight. I am sorry but it is not true. The health tradeoffs are greater if you gain weight then continue to smoke. It is just a win, win swicthuation being a non-smoker.

What if you slip?

You have to realize there may be times that you slip and have a cigarette. Just think to yourself it is ok that I slipped, I will just go back and not have any more cigarettes. It was this type of thinking that helped me get through those times I did slip. I cannot say enough if I had just the different type of thinking I would not have made it this far. As I have mentioned earlier now is the time for you to rally up your support time. This I mean all of your friends, counselors and whoever is helping you thru this difficult time. Like me if you do slip up that's ok. Just don't give up. Let me put it to you this way, just as long as you keep on trying you are a winner. The only time I consider any one a loser is when they stop trying and give up. So I am telling you no matter if you take your last breath and don't give up you are still a winner. As you get thru your first month reward yourself. Your rewards can be small, medium or large. Treat yourself as you go thru each month as a non-smoker. Here are some things I did for myself as I made it thru these times. I would take myself out for dinner, buy some new music, or just go for a nice ride. It is important you do this for yourself. This makes you realize you have made it this far. Next thing you will know you will be able to take yourself on a vacation with all of the money you have saved by not smoking.

You can do it just do not give up. You are a winner. Congratulations!!

You are now a non-smoker

Ok now that you have made it being a non-smoker it is time for you to help someone else. Tell them how you did it, remember everyone is different. You can give them suggestion of how you did it. Let them listen to you then decide what will be best for them. Stay with them all the way you can. Support them all the way to the end. This is the end of a new beginning.

Support

1. Call 1800-QUIT-NOW (1-800-784-8669. They will be able to guide you on how you can get support.
2. Check out the National Cancer Institute's smokefree.gov. The website is www.smokefree.gov. you can also contact them at their Smoking Quit line at 1-877-44U-QUIT
3. Check where you work at. Some workplaces help for those who want to quit. Some may offer quit-smoking clinics and support on the job. Others may pay for outside programs for their workers

4. Your doctor may know about a quit-smoking program near you
5. Look for your nearest Nicotine Anymous support group or another type of support group that may help.

Credits

Smokefree.gov

Lungusa.org

cdc.gov

drugabuse.gov

Newdirectionsprogram.com

Nida.nih.gov

Martin Luther King

Dictionary.com

Picture Faith of a Mustard Seed www.cafepress.com

Have faith of a mustard seed and you will be a non-smoker.

"For I assure you: If you have faith the size of a mustard seed, you will tell this mountain, 'Move from here to there,' and it will move. Nothing will be impossible for you." — Matthew 17:20

www.cafepess.com

It's time to act!

Thetruth.com

Made in the USA
Las Vegas, NV
03 October 2023